Know Your Numbers

Hands Down
Counting by Fives

by Michael Dahl   illustrated by Todd Ouren

Special thanks to our advisers for their expertise:

Stuart Farm, M.Ed., Mathematics Lecturer
University of North Dakota, Grand Forks

Susan Kesselring, M.A., Literacy Educator
Rosemount-Apple Valley-Eagan (Minnesota) School District

PICTURE WINDOW BOOKS
Minneapolis, Minnesota

Managing Editor: Catherine Neitge
Creative Director: Terri Foley
Art Director: Keith Griffin
Editor: Christianne Jones
Designer: Todd Ouren
Page production: Picture Window Books
The illustrations in this book were prepared digitally.

Picture Window Books
5115 Excelsior Boulevard
Suite 232
Minneapolis, MN 55416
877-845-8392
www.picturewindowbooks.com

Printed in the United States of America.

Library of Congress Cataloging-in-Publication Data
Dahl, Michael.
Hands down : counting by fives / written by Michael Dahl ;
illustrated by Todd Ouren.
p. cm. — (Know your numbers)
ISBN 1-4048-0948-1 (hardcover)
ISBN 1-4048-1117-6 (paperback)
1. Counting—Juvenile literature. 2. Multiplication—Juvenile
literature. I. Ouren, Todd, ill. II. Title.

QA113.D334 2004
513.2'11—dc22   2004018431

Time for art class! Today we will be using our hands.

FIVE fingers make a happy handprint.

5

4

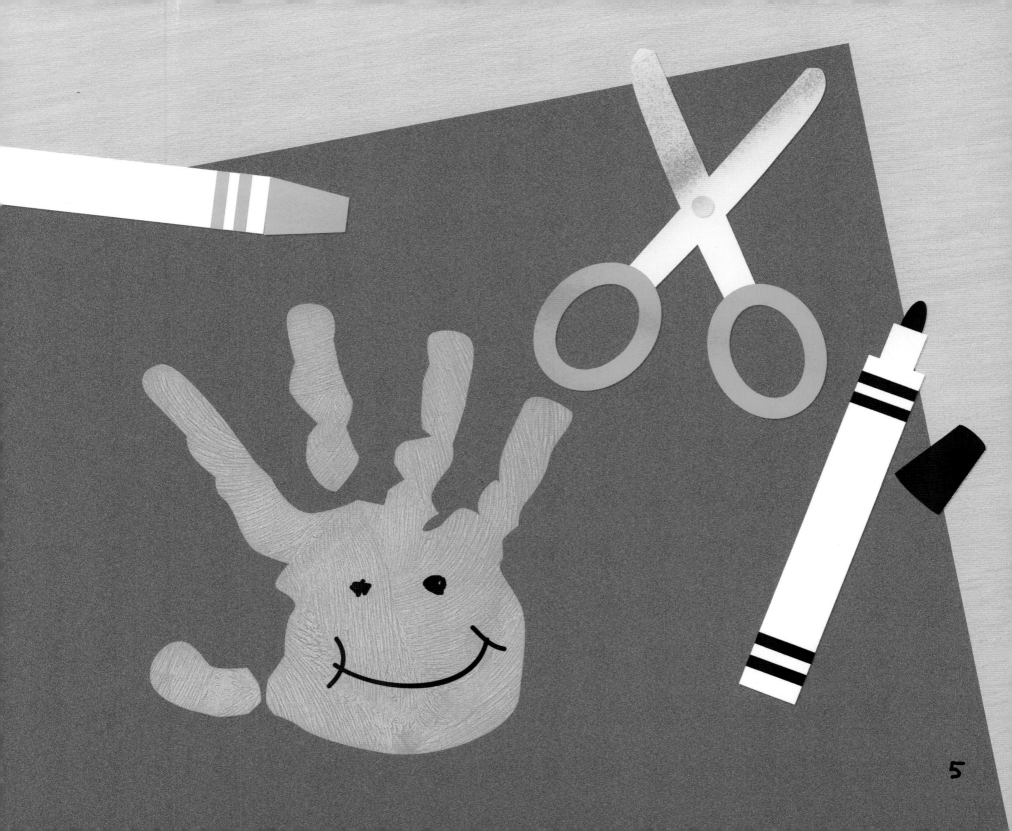

TEN fingers make a bright blue crab.

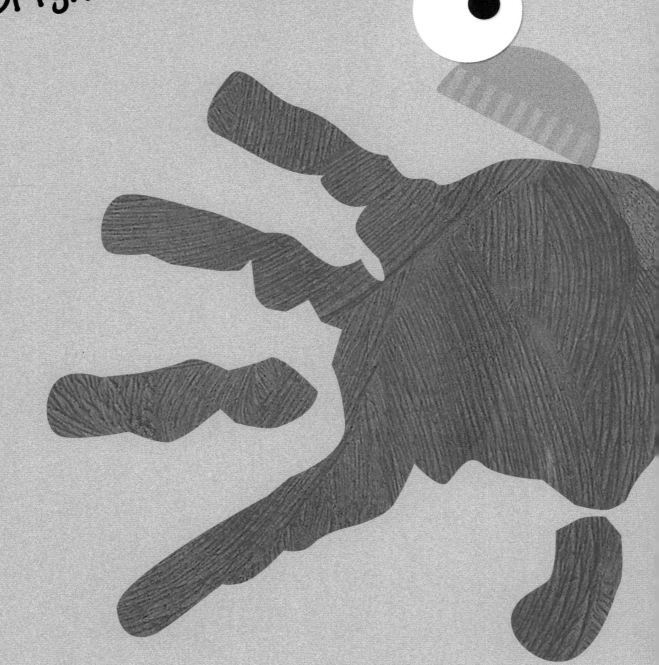

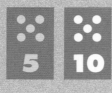

5   10

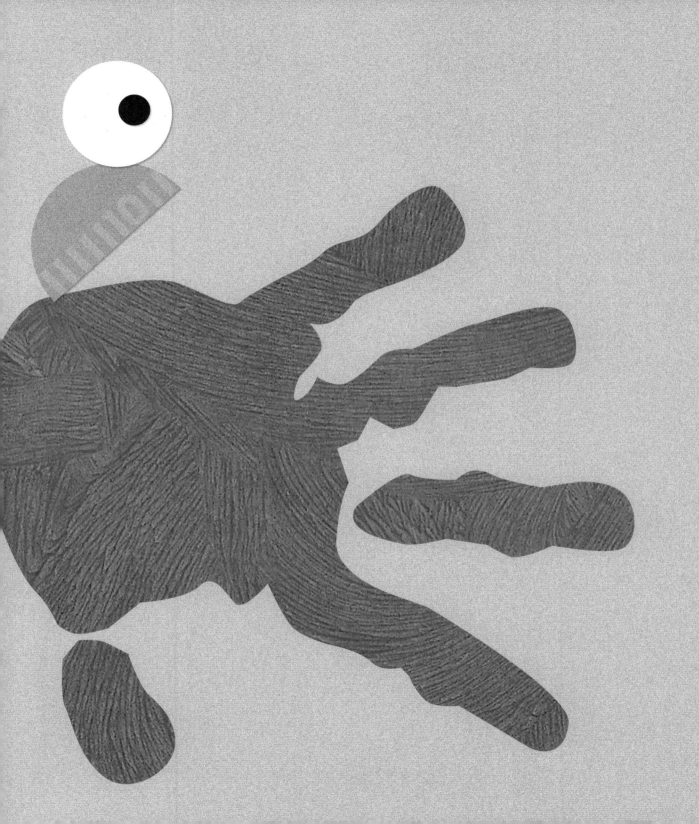

7

FIFTEEN fingers make lovely leaves on an old oak tree.

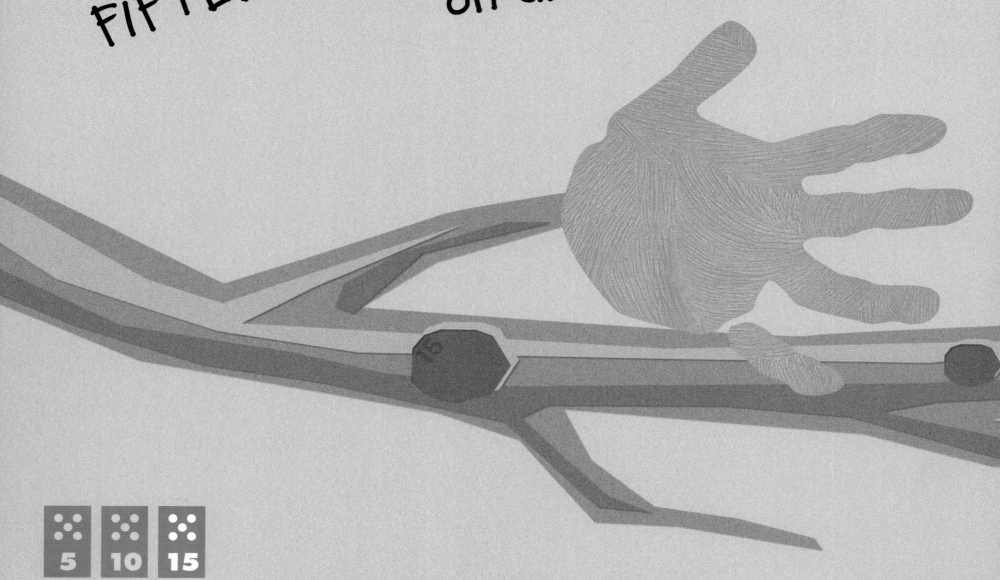

5 10 15

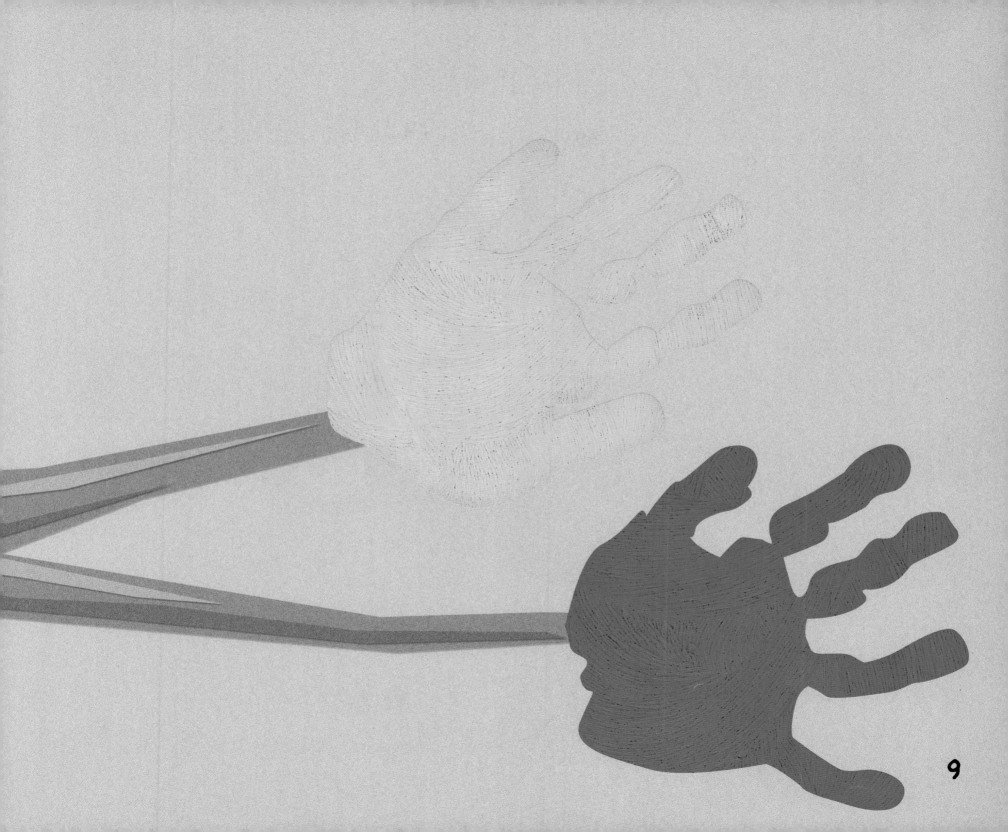

9

TWENTY fingers make beautiful butterflies.

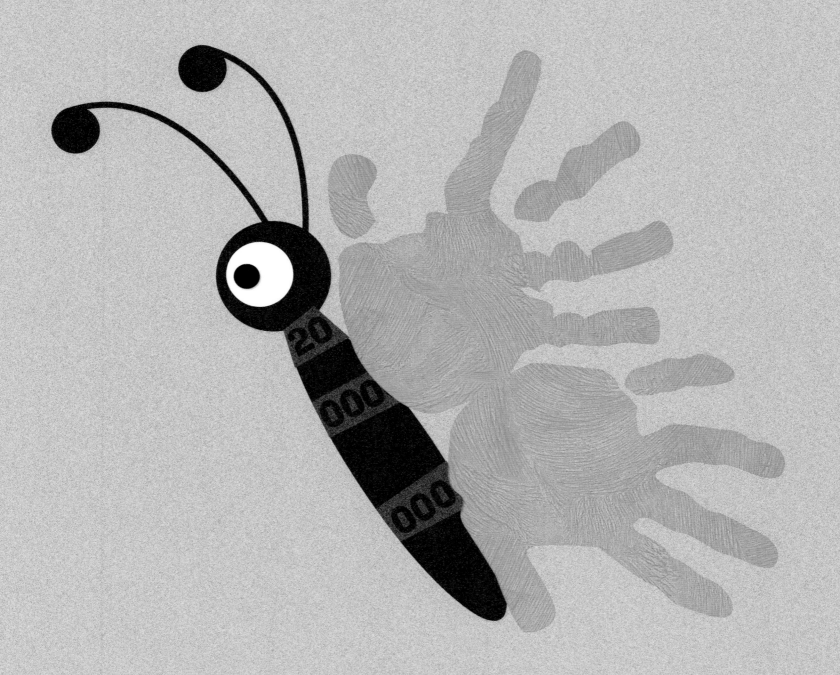

TWENTY-FIVE fingers make squiggly squid.

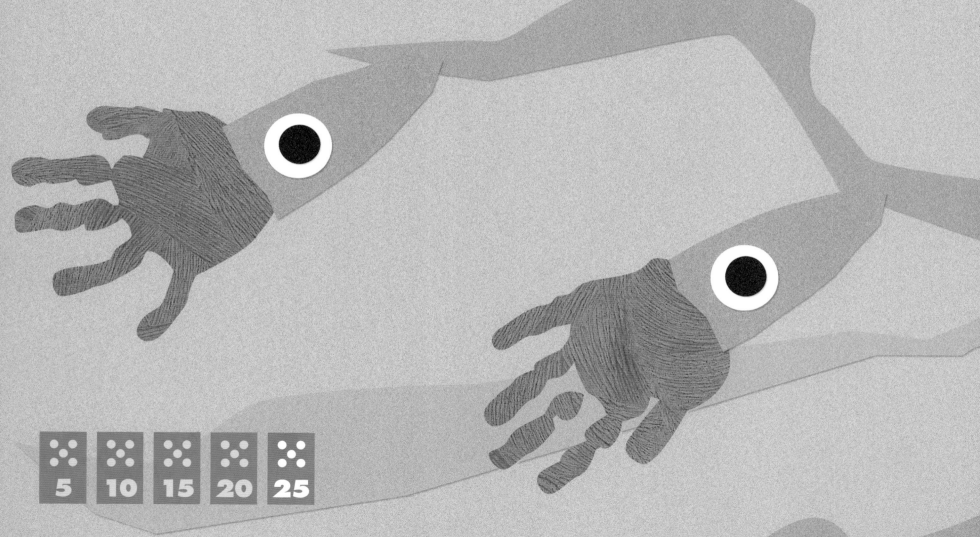

5 10 15 20 25

13

THIRTY fingers make kissing turkeys.

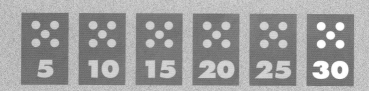

15

THIRTY-FIVE fingers make gloomy ghosts.

17

FORTY fingers make proud, prickly antlers.

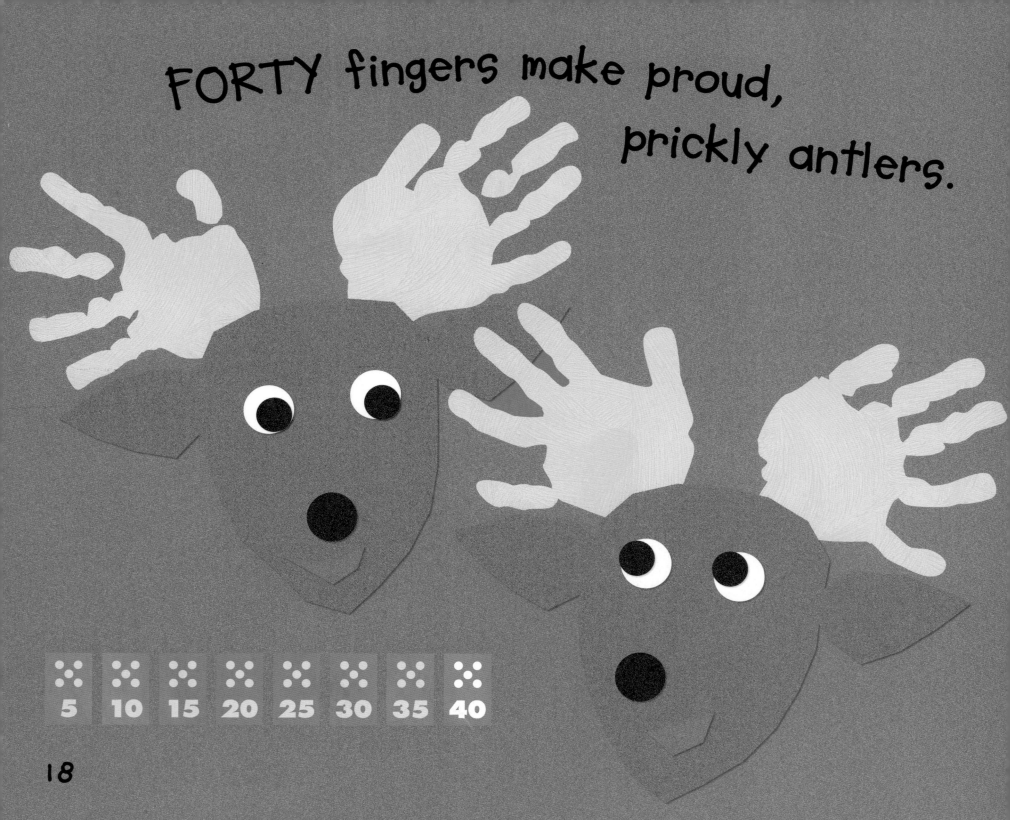

19

FORTY-FIVE fingers make a spectacular spring garden.

45

21

Jamal

Brynna

FIFTY fingers make a really cool art class.

Abbi

5 10 15 20 25 30 35 40 45 50